GEORGE HERBERT IN BEMERTON

From his bedroom windows George Herbert would have seen the Church to the front and the Rectory Gardens and River Nadder to the back

George Herbert in Bemerton

from Divine Landscapes
by Ronald Blythe

First published in the United Kingdom in 2005 by Hobnob Press
for the Summer Evenings with George Herbert Group and Bemerton Local
History Society, by kind permission of Ronald Blythe

Hobnob Press
PO Box 1838
East Knoyle
Salisbury SP3 6FA

British Library Cataloguing in Publication Data
A catalogue record for this book is available from the British Library.

ISBN 0-946418-41-1

Typeset in 12/16 pt Centaur, and Gill Sans
Typesetting and origination by John Chandler
Printed in Great Britain by Salisbury Printing Company Ltd, Salisbury

Illustrations

THROUGH THE YEARS there have been many engravings, sketches and postcards of the 'George Herbert Church' and the Old Rectory.

THE SOURCES for the historic views of Bemerton are illustrations taken from a number of nineteenth-century editions of George Herbert's work . Other illustrations, postcards and photographs are drawn from the archive of the Bemerton Local History Society, all donated by members of the Society.

THE PHOTOGRAPH of the chalice is by Chris Simpson and the interior view of St Andrew's is by John Chandler. Other present-day photographs are by local residents Roger and Clare Eagle. We are very grateful to all the contributors.

Introduction

OVER THE CENTURIES the people of Bemerton have celebrated the life and work of George Herbert, who was Rector from 1630 to 1633. In 2002 a group of local residents put on a series of summer events to celebrate George Herbert's life and writings. Actors, musicians, clergy, writers and local people took part and the following years have seen further events, including pilgrimage walks from Salisbury Cathedral to George Herbert's tiny church of St Andrew's.

ONE OF THE WRITERS taking part was Ronald Blythe, whose book *Divine Landscapes* contains a substantial chapter on Herbert. With the author's permission, for which we are most grateful, we are here reprinting that part of the chapter which covers Herbert's years at Bemerton.

DIVINE LANDSCAPES is a series of meditations on places in Britain rich in associations with prayer and spirituality. Chapter 6 is on George Herbert and the River Valley Route, and Blythe sees the poet being of both the earth and the spirit and says that Herbert hurries us to Christ as few other writers can.

WE KNOW OURSELVES to be part of a living tradition: we still use the bell that George Herbert tolled to call people to services and the key that he may have used to unlock the church door. It is a great privilege for us to live here, and to share the riches of Bemerton's 17th-century pastor and poet.

Simon Woodley, Rector of Bemerton
Judy Rees, Summer Evenings with George Herbert Group

Foreword

ALTHOUGH I COME from a different religious background, George Herbert's poetry has delighted and moved me since I first read it at the age of seventeen. Other than Izaak Walton's biography of Herbert, nothing has given me greater insight into his fruitful and too-brief journey through life than the biographical meditation by Ronald Blythe, an excerpt of which is printed here. I am grateful for its wit, its intensity of feeling, its enlightening juxtapositions, its clear yet complex structure and its decorous colloquiality, all very Herbertian attributes.

Vikram Seth
The Old Rectory, Bemerton
2005

St Andrew's Church Bemerton with George Herbert's Rectory on the right. The house is bigger than it would have been in George Herbert's time.

George Herbert comes to Bemerton

ONE OF THE CURIOUS THINGS about George Herbert, or perhaps about us, is this concentrating of him at the tail-end of his life in two small unremarkable buildings which face each other across a busy road, when nearly all the sites and scenes of his entire experience are still here for the savouring.

THE POPULAR NOTION of George Herbert, a writer who is increasingly accepted as England's principal devotional poet, is of a brilliant young seventeenth-century aristocrat who, after seeing his 'court hopes' dashed by the deaths of patrons, had some kind of spiritual crisis, turned his back on the world and became a simple clergyman. Albeit, a clergyman of literary genius. This has never been my view of him. I have always thought of him as someone for whom the delights of Christ had been obvious from childhood on, but that the especial glamour of his social position at Cambridge and the tempting possibilities of careers of all kinds quite naturally, given his youth, wit and protracted self-discovery, deflected him temporarily from a path which had been quite recognizable to him almost from the very beginning.

AND SO WE COME to Bemerton, Wiltshire, his brief parish, in order to be in a place where one of the most wonderfully written authentications of the discovery of the naturalness of the friendship of Christ was made.

ON 16 APRIL 1630 Herbert was presented by the Crown. ('Most willingly to Mr Herbert, if it be worth his acceptance,' agreed Charles I, voicing the general surprise that such a man should apply for such a living. Being much at home at Wilton House, the king could have been familiar with these two forlorn little chapels and their ruined rectory.) On 26 April, St Mark's tide, Herbert was taken first to Fugglestone and then to Bemerton by the Bishop of Salisbury and, although he was still only a deacon, inducted. The astonishment which his friends felt when they looked through the windows of St Andrew's, Bemerton, to find out what was keeping him, and then to discover him prostrate before the altar, only proves to illustrate into what a mere convention the ceremony had fallen. He was thirty-seven and amazingly happy. In the two years left to him

St Peter's Church Fugglestone.
Services are still held weekly here
in Fugglestone and in Bemerton

St Peter's Church Fugglestone. Services are still held weekly here in Fugglestone and in Bemerton

he was to give these churches and their rectory, which at that moment was uninhabitable, a significance that makes them a watershed in Britain's Christian history.

BEMERTON IN PARTICULAR conveys to perfection the Anglican definition of a shrine, which is a spotless structure for listening to words in. Nobody from Herbert's day to our own first sees it without receiving something of a shock. The church now clings stubbornly to what is not much more than a traffic peninsula, and Herbert's tiny village is now Salisbury's largest suburb. His initials twist and flash above the weathercock but the single bell in the turret which tolls against the roar of cars and lorries is that which tolled for his services.

The south door is the one which he opened and the chalice that from which he and his country communicants drank. Yet excessive care over the years has had the effect of obliterating the object which had to be cared for. The poet himself lies somewhere beneath the parquet and with the minimum of a memorial, as he required it, just a ceramic tile with a cross and 'G.H. 1632'. In a way it would have amused him, this carrying out his injunctions on cleanliness and neatness, and polishing him out of sight. A middle-aged man repairing the churchyard fence who couldn't help observing that I had arrived at an important destination, had to ask why I was there, at Bemerton. He excused his ignorance by telling me that he came from the New Forest.

"A poet named George Herbert used to be rector here."

"George Herbert," he said slowly, having never said it before. Then "Lately?"

"Oh, no. A long time ago."

"I don't read a lot," he said.

I PRAISED HIS FENCE, which was worth praising.

VANS AND CARS manipulated the chevron of roads created by the churchyard, and any procession from the house to chancel at ten and four today would need to be cautious. The

The chalice once used by George Herbert is now on display in the Chapter House of Salisbury Cathedral

Schoolchildren and traffic negotiate the narrow road

propinquity of Herbert's home to his altar still makes its point in spite of the traffic, and the site of those regular steps across the lane seems to be more protected than obliterated by tarmac. Bemerton means 'the town of the trumpeters'. Could it have been a music school for Old Sarum? What a sound by the river!

I know the wayes of pleasure, the sweet strains,
The lullings and the relishes of it;
The propositions of hot bloud and brains;
What mirth and musick mean; what love and wit
Have done these twentie hundred yeares, and more. . .

SO THIS IS THE SPOT where he set up and briefly delighted in his own holy household after a lifetime of belonging to institutions and being a peregrinating family guest. This is where he laid down his sacred version of the domestic law so 'courteously', as he would have described it, that what happened here between 1630 and 1633 vibrates in the imagination to this day. Herbert's household consisted of himself and his young wife, his three teenage nieces who had recently been orphaned, two men servants and four maids. Together they made an impressive group for him to lead across the lane twice a day for prayer and song. On the other side of the rectory lay his long medicine-chest of a garden, the River Nadder and a view of Salisbury Cathedral. Both the rectory fig tree and medlar are traditionally said to be his, and the prospect which he would have seen from his bedroom window is little changed. He taught, he preached – though not one of his highly popular sermons remains. Most of his parishioners were ordinary field-workers, 'thick and heavy, and hard to raise to a point of zeal, and fervency, and need a mountain of fire to kindle them . . .', so rather than attempt to whip them up by means of dramatic

The Rectory seen from the River Nadder, engraving by Gideon Fidler, 1880

oratory, Herbert's method was to 'give them stories and sayings they will remember'. Had not Christ done exactly this? The poet never preached for more than an hour and he always tried to preach 'something worth learning'. He insisted on kneeling and silence during prayers, and he deliberately created a profound atmosphere in his church by the manner in which he moved and spoke. It was his unaffected mixing of high solemnity and the practical and workaday which beguiled his congregation, who came to love his Matins and Evensongs so much that they would tie up their ploughs to the hedges when his bell rang and hurry to hear him, just as they were. Making it his 'business', a word he liked, to know all he could about agriculture and the ordinary working-life of the countryside, he seems to have established a genuine authority towards his people.

DURING HIS LAST MONTHS Herbert completed his 'Rule' for Britain's country clergy. In it, quite plain to see, although *en passant*, his own living of Fugglestone-with-Bemerton, exactly as it must have been when he took it in hand in 1630, reveals itself, warts and all. Only a country rector of his unselfconscious sanctity (Herbert insisted that holiness was much more a normal, rational requirement than a rare achievement) would have had the nerve to compose such a 'Rule' when he himself was so new to the job. This and the fact that he was now a priest in a hurry. Although never more perfectly alive, death was at his heel. There could be no settling down to leave his special godly mark, as some good rectors did. His had to be a fleeting incumbency whose imprint would be of another sort. A century of reformation, plus many centuries of folk attitudes, had obscured the nature of the priest of Christ and before Herbert encountered death, no longer ghastly but

> *gay and glad,*
> *As at dooms-day;*
> *When souls shall wear their new array,*
> *And all thy bones with beauty shall be clad*

he intended to reinstate this familiar and oft-derided village figure as a sacred force. Fugglestone-with-Bemerton would not be able to look back (although it did) on his brief pastorate as they would have on some dutiful shepherd who, as they say in Suffolk, 'had wintered us and summered us' for generations, but the English Church itself might live because he had lived. In order to illustrate a priest's common rural experience, Herbert drew on what he saw on his rounds near Salisbury, what he heard, what he himself actually did. *A Priest to the Temple* is thus an autobiography as well as a tough analysis of his flock. A highly unsuitable flock, it would seem, for a sickly, patrician man of letters. But in his 'Rule' the poet is indifferent to the suitability of parishes for certain types of clergymen. Wherever they are, in whatever kind of society, they have to be nothing less than 'the deputies of Christ for the reducing of man to the

Jason Battle's statue of George Herbert, placed at the West Front of Salisbury Cathedral in 2003

obedience of God'. And since being a priest of Christ is the ultimate honour attainable by man, an ordinary, sincere village clergyman, although the simplest of people, is equal to the sophisticated divines of the university and palace. At the end all that he needs to say, as Christ did, is, 'I sat daily with you teaching in the Temple.'

IT IS A DRAMATIC WAY of foreshortening time to read *A Priest to the Temple* at Bemerton and Fugglestone. Motorways recede and river-valley tracks and lanes take up the old ground. Three

Izaak Walton tells a story of George Herbert on his way to Evensong at the Cathedral. On one occasion he became a Good Samaritan to a poor man whose horse had fallen under its load

temples, Salisbury Cathedral, Bemerton chapel and Fugglestone church, and a palace, Wilton, give the local scale as Herbert would have known it. The voices along this route are his most eloquent ones and those of the rich and poor – chiefly the latter – which fill his book. T. S. Eliot wrote about 'the spiritual stamina of his work' and when Herbert says that a country parson has to care for his people 'as if he had begot the whole parish', this strength is demonstrated. Here is no detached moralist and kindly welfare worker but a father in God upon whom every child in God in his parish depends for its spiritual nourishment. They are an earthy, materialistic lot, these toilers of the fields which still break up the house plots of modern Salisbury, and 'because country people live hardly, and therefore as feeling their own sweat, and consequently knowing the price of money', their priest has to be 'exceeding exact in his life' and 'an absolute master and commander of himself'. It is crucial that he does nothing to 'the dishonour of his person and office'. He has to be 'not witty, or learned, or eloquent, but Holy'. He, of course, was all four in one and could not be otherwise. We catch a glimpse of the rectory interior, fresh as a Vermeer. It has to be the house beautiful on which all Fugglestone's and Bemerton's houses should be modelled, its furniture 'very plain, but clean, whole and sweet as his garden can make it' (herbs and cut flowers), and with Christ's words painted on their walls. In them, time must be found from all the field and housework to read and write, sing and, most particularly, for prayer.

HERBERT, IT COULD BE SAID, brought this place to its knees with disciplines and pleasures which few of his people would have previously associated with praying, and his elevation of prayer to the peaks of human activity makes uncomfortable reading for the average worshipper now. It needs much more time than we can spare for it. 'Hurry is the death of prayer,' says Francis de Sales, but it isn't hurry that is our weakness but our ignorance of how to direct time towards timelessness. This is what Herbert taught his little community to do, even if its time was not much more than seasonally varied dawns and dusks, 'I value prayer so,' he said,

> *That were I to leave all but one,*
> *Wealth, fame, endowments, venues, all should go;*
> *I and dear prayer would together dwell,*
> *And quickly gain, for each inch lost, an ell*

KNEEL IN ST ANDREW'S, BEMERTON, and imagine what kind of Christian worship was conducted in this temple by a rector who had declared himself on prayer thus:

> *Prayer the Churches banquet, Angels age,*
> *Gods breath in man returning to his birth,*
> *The soul in paraphrase, heart in pilgrimage,*
> *The Christian plummet sounding heav'n and earth;*

Engine against th'Almightie, sinners towre,
Reversed thunder, Christ-side-piercing spear,
The six-daies world transposing in an houre,
    A kind of tune. which all things heare and fear;

    Softnesse, and peace, and joy, and love, and blisse,
Exalted Manna, gladnesse of the best,
Heaven in ordinarie, man well drest,
    The milkie way, the bird of Paradise,

Church-bels beyond the starres heard, the souls bloud,
The land of spices; something understood.

THE COUNTRY PARSON, he insisted, 'has a special care of his church, that all things there be decent . . . walls plastered, windows glazed, floor paved, seats whole, firm and uniform, especially that the pulpit, and desk, and Communion Table, and Font be as they ought. . .' Unfortunately – if one can use such a word of criticism – this part of Herbert's Rule has been obeyed over and over again at Bemerton, so much so that one is stunned by the sheer mercilessness of this 'special care' which has carpented and plastered most of what he cared for out of existence. However, here it is, the holy room in which the ploughmen and better sorts crowded, and where he stood with arms extended, uniting them in 'a kind of tune', in 'the land of spices', offering them 'a banquet', leading them to 'where God's

breath would return to them', the thoroughly hallowed little building in which for a year or two he sang and coughed, a reassembled essence of the faith as he understood it. Here, at the east end, his coffin was placed under the floor on Quinquagesima Sunday, the Epistle for which has St Paul looking through a glass darkly and speaking of tongues ceasing. Herbert understood.

> *A man that looks on glasse,*
> *On it may stay his eye;*
> > *Or, if he pleaseth, through it passe,*
> *And then the heav'n espie.*

COULD THE GLASS which held his attention have been a medieval window through whose art he could stare into the blue sky beyond? Both images of the eternal would have delighted him. It was correct behaviour in church to dream yourself into and through both man and God's creations. He is the poet of gratitude. There was so much on which to 'stay his eye' that both his poetry and his rule for English country clergymen contain an underlying commentary and description of the places and objects which a loving and witty providence had, for a little under forty years, strewn around him for his 'pleasure'. Commons, enclosures, apples, pears and grapes, 'great estates' and 'stately habitations', churches everywhere, of course, and architectural detail, especially windows, flowers, trees, grasses

A modern-day view of St Andrew's interior

and 'greennesse', horses, sheep, birds, gardens, parks and courts, and 'bushy groves', hills and valleys and 'sweet walks', clouds, dew, rain and always the sun, 'these are thy wonders, Lord of Love'. Herbert celebrates an England which he believed God had made 'a land of Light, a storehouse of treasures and mercies', and his work ceaselessly tracks down every link it can between earthly experience and paradise. It is the poetry of a blessed continuum, with Wiltshire sprawling, quite naturally, across the frontiers of heaven. At Dauntsey, Edington, Baynton, Fugglestone, Bemerton and, twice a week at Salisbury, Christ the King was present with the poet in a close companionship whose subtleties amused them both. Who was guest, who host? Herbert's genius, almost four hundred years later, is to let us see the imprints of their parochial travels, and to listen to their intimate conversations. He asks, his God answers; the country sounds and sights penetrate their holy talk. Bells, lutes and trumpets play to delight them both. Divine love animates this world and the next. Riding up the old Roman Way to the north of Bemerton, and out on to Salisbury Plain, was often a giddy business, as creation and Creator sped through his intelligence. On his way he would have seen 'his flock most naturally as they are, wallowing in the midst of their affairs', and made them, if only for a few minutes, look up, which is not something which land-engrossed sheep, whether human or quadruped, are much given to doing. But he would have approved 'the great aptness of country people for thinking that all things come by a natural

Myles Birket Foster's Cathedral view to accompany a Victorian edition of Herbert's verse

cause...' Their Saviour too, as it happened. On the lower levels of Old Sarum he would have smiled at the 'cock-sure farmers' and on the summit amidst the ruins have felt his broken lungs working a bit more easily in the fine air.

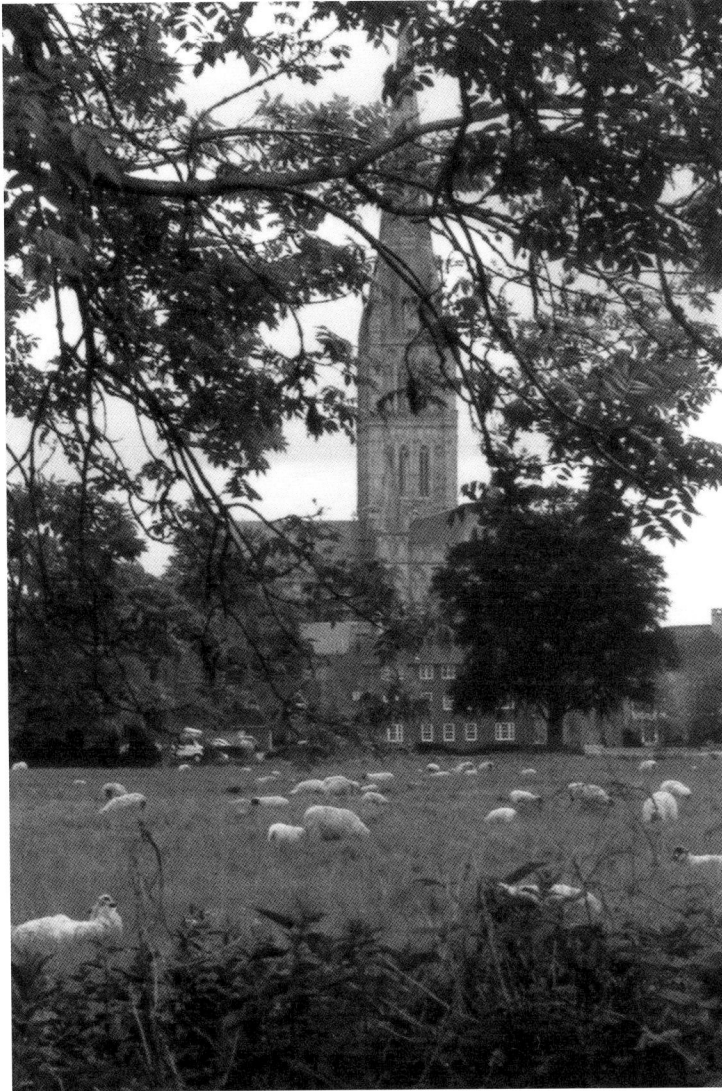

Some of God's wonders: the water meadows, grazed by sheep, and the Cathedral. The view is timeless.

And those who come after

THE CONTRAST of Herbertian simplicity at Bemerton and Herbertian splendour at Wilton provides perennial lessons. Those who have come a long way to see the shrine will go on to see the Pembrokes' palace and, what with Stonehenge and Salisbury Cathedral adding their uniquely influential contributions to the local scene, one soon sees that the great Christian poet reached the end of his own way of perfection in the context of some extraordinary neighbouring power centres. I, too, joined the conducted tour round Wilton House. It is a successful essay in magnificence, very grand, very beautiful. Sir William Chambers's triumphal arch topped by an equestrian Marcus Aurelius – 'The universe is transformation; our life is what our thoughts make it' – is the opposite of that 'unenriched' arch at Dauntsey and prepares one for what follows, which is as much richness as walls can take. The effect is one of richly dulling gold. We crocodiled, as thousands do all summer long, past the Van Dycks and Rembrandts, the Inigo Jones swags and Kent and Chippendale furniture. Past objects which could have been witnessed in Italy by Marcus Aurelius and, in England, by George Herbert. At the end, ungratefully, it must have sounded, having been shown so much, I asked our guide if there was anything of Herbert's to be seen? 'No.' Her answer was final and unapologetic. Had she not shown us art out of mind and glory beyond compare, domestically speaking? Not to mention more than enough to keep us going in the intimate sense, a lock of Elizabeth I's gingery hair, wan at the roots, an actual chair from the Roman senate, letters, telling little odds and ends which smelt of their owner's brief hour, rather than of posterity? However, if it is true, it does seem a serious omission. Impossible to imagine a continental princely house with a saint in the family not placing him above the decor and this world's achievements.

IN AUGUST 1865 the poet William Cory ('Heraclitus') was a guest at Wilton House and although he approved the social concern of the Pembrokes – 'the wealth here is flowing freely over the estates' – and found the luxuries of 'this famous palace' more defensible than those of King's College, Cambridge, he left a sharply critical account of George Herbert's little world, then just beginning to attract the modern pilgrim. It has always

Portrait of George Herbert in stained glass, in the west window of St Andrew's, Bemerton

intrigued me, because it has a claim to be amongst the first comments of the modern tourist to this holy place.

'AUG. 6. AT 5 P.M. I walked in the grounds alone; stepped the circumference of the ilex at the south-west corner of the house – eighty paces of shadow. . . I think I should get tired of this flat valley, where the magnificent timber hides the hill, and there is no sky, very little air, no sense of infinity. . . Aug. 8. At noon, A. called at our school-room and marched me off by appointment to Bemerton.' On the way we saw the new church, St John's, designed by T. H. Wyatt in 1860 and, not yet containing its pretty mosaic of Herbertian medlar trees, the work of Nellie Warre the rector's daughter.

"This isn't George Herbert's church," said the elderly village woman who was cleaning it to me. "It is a Victorian church. But it is a good example."

SHE WAS AN EXAMPLE of that legion of countrywomen who, more than any other group, and certainly more than the restorers, have been housekeepers to Christ in the best way possible, caring for his temples much as they care for their own homes, dusting and polishing, setting out flowers and maintaining works of art unawares. All the same, this is George Herbert's church so far as the nineteenth-century Pembrokes were concerned. They built it as 'a monument of so excellent a man, a renowned poet, a chaste priest, a good citizen', and I think he would have been surprised and delighted by it. William Cory was not delighted by it, as he saw it glaring in its newness five years after its consecration. It is 'all very well, though the tower is too dumpy'. But this criticism was as nothing when he saw Bemerton. Here he seethed with indignation. His is an all too rare glimpse of what a cultivated and spiritual mid-Victorian felt when coarse restoring hands got to work on an ancient edifice. 'But the old church George Herbert's church, is almost destroyed. There are a few ribs of the roof, stumps of windows, a floor heaped with rubbish. They may call it "restoration" if they like. At the parsonage the wife showed us the trees which Dyce drew for the picture of Herbert meditating: one is a medlar which the good man planted close to the pleasant little river – its trunk was coated with lead.' Later, he saw 'a go-cart stopping for a flock of sheep' which 'kicked up no dust, owing to the rain, and their valuable feet made pretty rakings and harrowings over the dark soft roads'. Herbert would have liked that 'valuable feet'.

> *The shepherds sing; and shall I silent be?*
> *My God, no hymn for thee?*
> *My soul's a shepherd too; a flock it feeds*
> *Of thoughts, and words, and deeds.*
> *Thy pasture is thy word: the streams, thy grace*
> *Enriching all the place.*

Shepherd and flock shall sing, and all my powers
Out-sing the day-light hours.

NO PRETTY RAKINGS and harrowings over the dark soft
Bemerton roads now, but the Salisbury meat lorries hurtling
past 108 Lower Road, or Herbert's rectory. And yet and yet, the

Myles Birket Foster's view of St Andrew's Bemerton

pastures, the stream, there they are still, limpid and maintaining their damp paths to the right, and stretching onwards as they did in his time to the edge of the city. As he walked to the Cathedral to join the choir twice a week, these and the Lower Road would have been his composing tracks, those regular strolling places where poetry works itself out. Edward Thomas, describing the Herbert landscape beyond Wilton, the 'waved green wall of down, the castle among the marsh-marigolds of the flat green meadows, the moorhen hurrying down the swift water, the bulging wagons of straw going up a deep lane to the sheep-folds. . . A trap weighted with two ordinary men and a polished, crimson-faced god of enormous size drove off Lord Pembroke's cart followed, full of dead hares. . .' would have understood.

NOT ENTIRELY SURPRISINGLY, since his wife had a cottage in Winterslow, William Hazlitt, a Christ-respecting agnostic, adds his description of Herbert's countryside just at the same time as Constable painted it.

> I remember once strolling along the margin of a stream, skirted with willows and plashy sedges, in one of those low sheltered valleys in Salisbury Plain, where the monks of former ages had planted chapels and built hermits' cells. There was a little parish church near; but tall elms and quivering alders hid it from my sight, when, all of a sudden, I was

The tradition of celebrating George Herbert in Bemerton continues startled by the sound of a full organ pealing on the ear, accompanied by rustic voices, and the willing quire of village-maids, and children. It rose, indeed, 'like an exhalation of rich distilled perfumes.' The dew from a thousand pastures was gathered in its softness; the silence of a thousand years spoke in it. . . It filled the valley like a mist. . .

The Effigies of Mr George Herbert,
Author of those Sacred Poems called
The Temple.

What Church is this? Christ's Church. Who builded it?
Master George Herbert. Who assisted it?
Many assisted: who I may not say,
So much contention might arise that way.
If I say Grace gave all; Wit straight doth thwart,
And says, All that is there is mine: but Art
Denies, and says, There's nothing there but's mine:
Nor can I easily the right define.
Divide: say, Grace the matter gave, and Wit
Did polish it. . . ;
In building of this Temple, Master Herbert
Is equally all Grace, all Wit all Art.
Roman and Grecian muses all give way:
One English poem darkens all your day.

HERBERT'S POETRY is about what Christ himself called 'the temple of the living God', the human body; its earthly lodgings and its house of prayer. It can thus be seen as a poetry of total landscape involving all divine and human creativity, all nature and all art. It is still the best spiritual guide to an English place.

Ronald Blythe's book Divine Landscapes *was published by Viking in 1986*
His selection from George Herbert's writings A Priest to the Temple or The Country Parson, with selected poems *was published by Canterbury Press, Norwich in 2003.*